The Attitude of Faith

The Attitude *of* Faith

RALI NTUWISENI RALIKHUVHANA

AuthorHouse™ UK
1663 Liberty Drive
Bloomington, IN 47403 USA
www.authorhouse.co.uk
Phone: 0800.197.4150

Published by AuthorHouse 02/04/2015

ISBN: 978-1-5049-3572-2 (sc)
ISBN: 978-1-5049-3573-9 (e)

CONTENTS

MY QUOTES

'The employment of the right attitude will make your desired altitude. I employ the attitude of faith then'

'I love Love'

'God's love was given with love'
'Love is an instrument; it just has to be used cleverly'

DEDICATION

I dedicate this book to my late pastor, brother and friend Mr Ndifelani Edward Nemubvumoni who died in a car accident of which I was a driver on the 28th day of January 2011.
Born 1972-2011
I shall remember him for his loving, giving, enduring and caring heart. His love for laughter and jokes, his friendship and commitment in God's work
May His soul rest in peace.

APPRECIATIONS

I wish to extend my sincere appreciations to my Senior Pastor, NM Makhado for the subject of faith, to which he introduced me very thoroughly. I now can transplant it in all manners. I thank you. God bless you and your families. You raised me to this which I have become, it was not easy I believe so but you did it so well. I thank you again. You led me to the ordained path whilst I was not fully conscious of it. Am glad I am this today. I wish to appreciate all the pastors who supports you in your mission as a leader, father and pastor of the Centre of Faith Bible church, to which I am a serious member. I thank the Midrand Assembly for being there for me at all the times, they make my job easy. Stay blessed, I love you all.

CHALLENGE

I wish to challenge my children and teach them that they have to create an altitude of their own. I love you all and equally so. I promise to always be the father that I am to you and be the children that you are to me. God bless you all.

SPECIAL APPRECIATIONS AND ACKNOWLEDGEMENTS

First of all, I am forever indebted to you oh God my creator. I wish I can say more but suffice to say thank you. Secondly, special thanks to my beautiful wife of one year, Katlego. I call you a blessing from God. Thanks a lot for your contribution to this book. I love you. My parents Luvhengo and my late father Masindi, and to my siblings Ndivhewafhi, Avhazwifuni and Thizwihangwi. I must not forget my teachers, all of you from primary to Secondary. To Steven Tshivhase and your friend Mmbenge Netshisaulu. You made me desire to write. Budeli Rofhiwa, Dowelani Netshisaulu, and Pastor M W Matodzi, all from Apostolic Unity Church. Pastor Mudau Ndikandafhi Rymond, thanks for your contribution to this book, Tshililo

Vele, Pastor Nnditsheni Mukhuba and Pas
Vele Livhuwani all from Centre of faith Bible
Church. Pastor Eunice Motsitsi of God is power
Ministries in Germiston, Jnb and Pastor Joel
Baloyi. Mr P Mphanama my retired and former
principal. Pastor Rasimphi and my father Pastor
Maupa Mokgola of Full Gospel Church.
I appreciate all the pastors who raised me, preached
to me and helped in my raising up and growth
in the understanding of the word of God.
To the Centre of Faith Bible Church
family and Rali Stars FootBall Club.

INTRODUCTION

The attitude of faith is what I want to talk about. I must say that I preached about this topic in our local church on the 13th day of July 2014. I felt a strong conviction to then book it up. I was also invited to a local community Radio station called The Voice of Tembisa, and preached about the same topic. This is how convicted I am of the topic. We must all know about this, the reason this book. It is an easy read.

I found that attitude is a settled way of thinking or feeling, a position of the body indicating a particular mental state. It is a self confident behavior. (*New 2nd Edition Oxford South African Concise Dictionary*)

Our continued talk will be easy when we understand these concepts. I now wish to define faith as per my dictionary.

Faith is a complete trust or confidence, a strong belief in a religion, based on spiritual apprehension rather than proof. (*New 2nd Edition Oxford South African Concise Dictionary*) This I say is the definition for the purposes of our subject.

It is important to note that once there is proof, it is not a matter of faith anymore. Faith seeks no proof. One's desire to want to see first and then believe is a clear sign that there is no faith in such a one. Jesus complained and He said: *see the book of John 20 from verse 24 to 29,* to summarize the text in my own words; *Thomas when told that Jesus was seen he answered and said until I see in His hands the print of the nails, and put my finger into the print and put the hand into his side, 'I will not believe'*

Thomas refused to believe and made demands as a pre-requisite to his believing. This the Lord does not want of us. We must believe before we see.

Then Jesus in verse 26 came to him whilst in the company of others. He ministered to Thomas and said to him; Thomas; *'reach your finger here, and look at my hands; and reach your hand here, and put it into my side. Do not be unbelieving, but believing.'*

Thomas said *'My Lord and my God!'*

Jesus said to him *'Thomas, because you have seen Me, you have believed. Blessed are those who have not seen and yet believed.'*

Thomas refused to believe before seeing, this isn't faith and God wants us to have faith.

In the book of Psalm 22 verse 16, we hear of the congregation of the wicked, wicked because of unbelief. They refused to believe. Jesus said prophetically that *'the congregation of the wicked has enclosed Me. They pierced My hands and My feet.'* Jesus was talking about them that killed Him. I would not like to be compared to them.

I plead with you not to be such as this congregation. Do not wait for Jesus to rebuke you. Do not fall short of His blessings first before you believe. Believe!

Thomas was lucky in that he believed before he died but as for the dogs, they did not. Believe now so that you do not die in your unbelief.

The word of God says that 'faith is the substance of things hoped for, the evidence of things not seen'. *Hebrew 11 verse 1.* Many say that this is a definition of faith but I will say that it gives a description of what faith does. Substance means essence or reality. Faith treats things hoped for as reality. Evidence means proof or conviction. Faith itself proves that what is unseen is real.

Faith is in itself more than proof. Those that await proof will have less but to them that believe already have more. Faith is by faith proof of the unseen. Those who do not believe are not blessed. Study the conversation between Jesus and Thomas you will apprehend even more.

Now the kind of faith we are talking about is what the word say faith comes by hearing and hearing by the word of God. Romans 10 verse 17. Faith is built on the word of God, not philosophy and experience. In our case not biology. Biology talks but one must make a choice as to whether to hear the voice of biology or that of God through His word. Nothing is impossible with God, yep, thou biology may seem to be very correct and loud in its talk. The word of God may seem to be very low and soft. It does not change what the word says God is, nothing is impossible with Him. Once you build your faith on the word of God, then and safely attitudinize. The attitude of faith, our main subject. It is all about the word of God, faith, prayer and attitude. Our learning reference will be Hannah.

THE CHALLENGED HANNAH

In essence the book of I Samuel Chapter 1 and 2 contains our reference in this regard, of importance in this section is I Samuel 1 verse 1, the word of God says that '*Now there was a certain man of Ramathaim Zophim, of the mountains of Ephraim, and his name was Elkanah the son of Jeroham, the son of Elihu, the son of Tohu, the son of Zuph, an Ephramite.*

In verse 2, it says that 'And *he had two wives: the name of one was Hannah, and the name of the other Peninnah. Penninah had children, but Hannah had no children'.*

In verse 3, the word says that 'this *man went up from his city yearly to worship and sacrifice to the Lord of hosts in Shiloh. Also the two sons of Eli, Hophni and Phinehas, the priests of the Lord, were there'.*

Verses 4 to 7 provide that '*And whenever the time came for Elikanah to make an offering, he would give portions to Peninnah his wife and to all her sons and daughters. But to Hannah he would give a double portion, for he loved Hannah, although the Lord had closed her womb. And her rival also provoked her severely, to make her miserable because the Lord had closed her womb. So it was, year by year, when she went up to the house of the Lord, that she provoked her; therefore she wept and did not eat*'.

It is important to take note of the following that the place they occupied and called home was a place given to them by God through Joshua, see Joshua 17 verse 17 to 18, the word of God says that 'And *Joshua spoke to the house of Joseph-to Ephraim and Manasseh-saying, "you are a great people and have great power; you shall not have only one lot, but the mountain country shall be yours. Although it is wooded, you shall cut it down, and its farthest extent shall be yours; for you shall drive out the Canaanites, though they have iron chariots and are strong."*

The land was an inheritance from God as per the promise during the time of Moses and was divided by Joshua. *Joshua 1: 6.*

The man of the mountains of Ephraim was not misplaced at all. It was God's given portion of land.

Again the man had two wives; they were all wives to him. It is important to understand that polygamy was no sin, (I do not suggest that it is at this age a sin) it was an accepted social custom throughout the ancient Middle East. Even in ancient Israel it was an accepted practice. The man of the mountains of Ephraim took a second wife for children since his first wife was a barren. He needed an heir, pride, maintenance of a place in the tribal allotments and preservation of a family name.

The man of the mountains of Ephraim went up from his city yearly to worship and sacrifice to the Lord of hosts in Shiloh.

See Joshua 18:1, Exodus 34:14, and Deuteronomy 12:5-7.

He did not go up to worship just another god but the Lord of hosts and this he did yearly as he should, together with his family. It must be understood that he was not obliged to take his family with yet he did. He did not take them with to be spectators, he gave to them portions to worship and sacrifice to the same God together with himself and others. He did a noble thing; what a man should do for his house. It is not a matter of saying as for me and my house we going to serve the Lord, no, be a model.

Despite the fact that Hophni and Phinehas were there, he never stopped attending to his duties with his family whenever the time came. He would go up to Shiloh to worship and sacrifice.

Remember the man of the mountains of Ephraim was able to solve his problem by marrying the second wife. The first wife's problem did not just remain it grew bigger and stronger. She was barren, secondly her husband brought home a rival and this functioned against her alone, so the problem grew bigger and sharper, ready to eat her up.

Despite the double portions from her husband, the challenge remained. It would even manifest more during the time of going up to worship and sacrifice to the Lord of hosts. The word of God says that in verse 6 *'and her rival also provoked her severely, to make her miserable, because the Lord had closed her womb'*

Her rival was correct in that indeed she was a barren, she provoked her with a purpose of making her miserable and she succeeded in doing so. When it happened Hannah would cry and not eat.

The man of the mountains of Ephraim would say to her *'why do you weep? Why do you not eat? And why is your heart grieved? Am I not better than ten sons?'* of course not, the husband could not be better than one son even. Children are important and Hannah needed one. Barrenness was one of the grounds for divorce at the time, it was also very clear that the problem was with her since her husband had children with the second wife. The husband could have divorced her, maybe she anticipated it. Who wants to live in such uncertainty? Thinking of the possible consequences is a burden on its own and I can't imagine what the poor woman was going through.

I wish I can talk to the husband; tell him that marriage is good if it has its fruits one of them being children. That the challenge Hannah had was not a husband, she had a loving, God fearing husband, a dream husband if I can say so but her challenge was not that but children. She received double portions to worship and sacrifice to God of hosts, that compensation served a different purpose and the gap she had just remained. It was painful, painful to the point of loss of appetite and crying. Hannah was soon going to be sick, lose weight and become ugly, divorce was lying ahead of her. She had to do something about her case.

It is not in much time where a husband means naught to a woman, this is what happened in Hannah's life. She had a husband, food, favour and love from her husband, respect and exposure and opportunities. There was but a great need in her heart. A child or children is all she needed. She was truly challenged.

Hannah experienced all of these whilst she was one of the children of God, she pleased God and was married, she went to offer her worship and sacrifice, she fought not with her rival, she was a godly person, yet she lacked a child, and it was painful. This was real.

Hannah was a woman of good faith, a matured woman. Just like the word which fell amongst thorns, Hannah was supposed to lose heart, to lose faith due to her situation. The situation was bad enough to negate her faith in God but not. Faith must be tested. Ones' faith must pass the test. Tests are meant for those who registered, taught, attended and are ready for a promotion. A wise learner cannot wish a test away. If you look at it, those who registered, attends and are taught seems to be good learners. The test is fortunately meant for them. Good learners. Your test fits you, face it. Your challenge fits you, challenge it back. God is your strength, you will make it.

The test is not for everyone. One must qualify to be tested. A test is therefore an opportunity to step up. It isn't an obvious opportunity. It is not meant for everyone. Take advantage of your test therefore. Hannah took advantage of hers. What about you, we can all do so and achieve more. When challenged you think witches, you blame it on God the Lord of hosts, what's wrong with you? When challenged you think of accusing someone. You are running this race by accident, step out. Disqualify yourself and there will be test no more upon your life. Tests and promotions are meant for good peoples, just like Hannah.

One may wonder what purpose the worship and sacrifices served in her life, obviously what we fail to apprehend. We saw that Hannah needed to focus on her challenge in an unusual way, she did it and when she did something too much came to pass. Hannah the mother of one of the major Prophets, Samuel.

It is amazing who our rivals are in real life. The Devil is the prime one but he uses peoples. The peoples that he uses are not far from us. They are in our bedrooms, kitchens, dining halls and so on. They are too close to us to know almost everything about us. Their job becomes even easy, effective and efficient.

Our rivals even dine with us. Judas was a treasurer at Jesus' church. He even dined with Jesus and other disciples. Their effectiveness depends on their proximity with us and our persons. Its effectiveness is not suppose to work against you but in your favour. The activities of your rival must make you instead.

Joseph in Genesis 50 verse 20 says *'But as for you, you meant evil against me; but God meant it for good, in order to bring it about as it is this day, to save many people alive.* In verse 21 he says *'Now therefore, do not be afraid; I will provide for you and your little ones.'*

Joseph was so much in charge of the problem which he did not form but his brothers. Not brothers from another father but same. Surname fought against itself here. Josephs' dreams and the evil role the brothers played were all equally important for the realization of the dreams he had, which made his brothers hate and resent him in the first place.

Hannah's rival was in the house. The more she inflicted pain on Hannah the more the passion and energy on the part on Hannah to want to solve the problem God's way. Remember our battle is not canal. We are not called to fight with people but the enemy and how we fight determines our victory. Who we fight with determines our victory too. When you fight God's battle you must be on your knees, believe in God. Remember He is the man in the battle field fighting our battles. We cannot have scars. Those with scars are fighting their own way and not God's way.

THE PLAN OF ACTION

Hannah made a vow and this was her way or dealing with her situation. The love of her husband was not enough, favours from her husband were not enough at all. The need remained until a plan or a vow was made to talk to God about it, told Him what she needed and how. She asked for a male child, not just a child.

She sought to pray about her problems ***See 1 verse 10.*** It is not impossible for anyone to pray. Just to have a conversation with God about that which is paining you. Talk about it with God. Tell it to God and tell Him what you want from Him. I believe that this is very simple. I encourage you to do it then. God awaits a conversation with His child, you, with you. Talk with Him.

I want you to understand that God is too good and we always benefit from making plans to converse with Him in that He walks our paths instead of meet us half way. Half way is too far for us, God knows that, the whole journey is impossible for us. We need Him all the way. I like Moses, he said '*if your presence does not go with us, do not bring us up from here*" in the book of Exodus 33 verse 15.

Zacchaeus made a plan to see Jesus but lo, Jesus took over and saw Mr Zacchaeus, asked him to step down. I tell you, Zacchaeus achieved more, for him it became a lifelong reward and not just something for a day. The dude just wanted to see who Jesus was, that's all. When Jesus took over; He saw him, asked him to come down, which he did. Stayed in his house. He received salvation and re-paid to them he had robbed.

The **lost son** made a plan to rather go back home and see his father. The word says that whilst he was still a great way off, his father saw him and had compassion, and ran and fell on his neck and kissed him and welcomed him home. Did he ever say all that which he planned to say to his father? Nope. The father just took over and the son achieved more.

I am but scared; if one reads Luke 15 verse 11 to 32 closely and number 27 to be specific, there the word of God says that '*your brother has come, and because he received him safe and sound, your father has killed the fatted calf.'*

There was a high possibility of receiving him unsafe and of no sound mind. The father heard the lad say in verse 21 that *'father, I have sinned against heaven and in your sight, and am no longer worthy to be called your son'*. I tell you, a person of unsound mind cannot utter such humble words. When he looked at him he saw a complete person and learnt that indeed his son was safe. He was complete; his body parts were all there. The reason he celebrated his return. Imagine if the lad had gone mad and incomplete? This lad was lucky, a return in this state is not guaranteed at all. Some when they return is for burial at home, apology prior to their death, a proper good bye to their family members, very sad it is.

Did the **four leprous men** know that God will strengthen them? They were rejected, placed by the gate of the city to die and not infect others. These are the people who came back to report the good news to the ruler at the time. These are the people that God used to fulfill the prophesy of the prophet Elisha, to direct victory to His own nation. It was done through four men who were sick with leprosy. Did they know that what happened was going to happen? I know they did not know. I tell you thou that they achieved more.

Ask yourself a question why am I seating here until I die. Do I die if I seek to speak with God? Needless to say, you do not die. Instead you die if you do nothing. Death as a result of inaction. I say you don't even have to wake up or stand up. Speak from your position. God will hear you, of all the people who are talking about your situation, God will hear you instead. Tell it all to Him, do so by yourself. He awaits you and once you decide to do it, like I said he will walk your paths. It will be doable for you.

Daniel in *Daniel chapter 1 verse 8*. The word says that he purposed in his heart, *in verse 9* thereof, the word shows us God's intervention promptly after purposing. Again I say God will never meet you halfway. He will take you through and your plan will work out just fine.

The plan Hannah made was not cheap but free. It was not heavy but simple. She didn't even have to be heard by human. She didn't speak out to the world but to God. She didn't voice it out to the whole church but to God. The Priest did not even hear. The Priest was there but heard nothing. He was not even told why he was there at that time, God knew that he was going to be there in order to bless and all of these happened after action, effort being a prayer.

Hannah was alone. Her challenge affected not only her but her husband too. She did not invite her husband. An invitation to her husband was going to be an invitation to employ another approach to her problem. She needed no comfort and advice; I think that's what she would have received had she invited her husband. In fact her husband tried to comfort her. It did not work. He even solved his problem by marrying a second wife.

I tell you now that if you do not step out and do something very simple with your situation, you will soon become part of the situation. You will soon turn into a proverb and a monument. I would not want to be a negative reference in learning, would you? Do something about your situation, do it now. Faith is now, today, this time. Just talk to your father, our God. That's all I prescribe, nothing more.

Hannah acknowledged that she had a challenge and she decided to talk to God about it. It worked, she received more. I tell you now that if she had consulted people, to the extent of asking for a child from people, she would have received one child. She talked to God, the almighty God, she received more. She asked for a child and she became a mother of six children. Hannah received more. This is the kind of God I serve and talk about herein. Ask Him, believe and you will receive whatever you ask. He meet our needs for He knows what we need before we even ask Him. What are you waiting for; He waits to meet your needs.

The plan Hannah made. In verse 1:10, *the word of God says that 'and she was in bitterness of soul, and prayed to the Lord and wept in anguish'.*

How many of us would when challenged by the harsh realities of this life think like Hannah did? Her husband's love was not enough and could not fill the gap of not having children, and the pain caused by her rival. She made a choice of talking it all to God her creator and she did so in her human position, in her state of hurt. The bible says that she cried bitterly and such a cry was not fake but real. In that state she prayed, the reason her prayer was to humans weird. In her state of both mental and physical pain she spoke with God and He heard her. God samueled her. There are many other things she could have done to make herself feel better but thanks to God for she chose a path that gave her permanent results as opposed to temporary. If you were in her position wouldn't you have dealt with your rival physically or seek to bewitch or poison her children so as to permanently get rid of her pride? The results were going to be very canal; in fact you would be in the same position as your rival. God has more for you. He wants you to lead your rival and not equal you with him or her.

Focus not on your rival and seek God. God will put your rival in her position and once that happens you shall take your possessions and your position.

Seek God now before you get better. Desire Gods' solution.

I tell you now that Hannah's challenge needed no men but God only. A proper reading of chapter 1 verse 13 reveals that her challenge needed no one but God only. The word of God says that *'Now Hannah spoke in her heart; only her lips moved, but her voice was not heard. Therefore Eli thought she was drunk'*

The prophet of the Lord did not know, did not even hear. Prophets don't think, they prophesy, Eli thought and he thought wrong. This was for God and to God. Hannah's voice was not heard but God heard it. *'She said give me a male child and I will give him to the Lord for the rest of his life'.*

Rise up and pour your heart to God and not to a human like you and me. We all do have limitations but God lacks same. When you already know what the challenge is then seek God not a prophet, seek no counsel but the face of God the father.

Don't prepare yourself, go to God in your state, confused as you are, dirty as you are, bitter as you are, down as you are, go don't stop.

This time Hannah did not offer animals, just the words which only she and God heard. It was not even another trip; she just took her corner and talked with God, alone. Remember they all went up there to worship and sacrifice, she then stepped out to pray for her own challenges. Step out, some would say launch into the deep, take one step out like Jesus and see the impact of your personal decision, the impact of your personal experience with God the Almighty. It is always different and results are inevitable.

Pour out your heart before the Lord and He will gather it, clean it up and fill it up to the brim.

Make a plan to meet the Lord the God of hosts and He will take over. The desired results will surely come upon you.

I must say that if we decide not to take action, depending on our position; if standing, the solution is under our feet, if seating, we seating on our solution. If we rise up and if we take a walk it will be seen. I encourage you to take action.

THE ATTITUDE HANNAH PUT ON

We are talking about the right attitude in order to achieve the desired altitude. The attitude which is informed by faith, faith from the word of God of hosts. I am very much impressed by the attitude that Hannah adopted in this regard.

We see the type of a problem Hannah had, its effect on her life but not faith. She prayed and believed that her prayer was heard and as such had worked.

I am a believer that without faith emptiness and lack will prevail and reign. This is absolutely no life ordained by God. In fact the word of God says that God is not pleased by one without faith. Faith is the receiving hand; it only receives from God and not men.

Attitudinize if you have prayed. If you are a woman put on some clean clothes, some make up, do your nails and hair. Put on a smile. Walk, talk, lift your head up and walk the walk. Be seen, be heard. Be active again. Go back to work. Put on your best clothes. Eat and drink again. Revert to your routine. Put on your confidence again. Take a long bath. Visit your Pastor or spirit filled friend, talk about His promises to His own.

Let them wonder and want to know, some may say that same problem which according to their canal observation is still there but you act as if it isn't there anymore; he is crazy as a result. Start a chorus in your home cell or at the Christians' gatherings. Greet people, and if you are a woman, walk like a woman not like a man. Be sure of where you are going, no frustrations anymore. They will ask 'what happened? And you will say, the Lord remembered me.

He is the prince of peace, allow the peace of talking to Him reign. Conversations with God are meant to give you peace. The reason she did not war against her rival. Prayer of faith brings forth peace, perfect peace. Enduring peace.

In the midst of the load and cloud that befall Hannah, there was love and favour from her husband. There was God to run to. God did not give her what was more than enough for her to carry. In addition to that there was the peace of God.

See Philippians 4: 6 to 7. In 7, the word of God says that *'and the peace of God, which surpasses all understanding, will guard your hearts and minds through Christ Jesus.'* Once you shall have made your request known to God the Lord of hosts then you shall peace up and there will be no efforts and struggle on your part to do so. It will happen since you have prayed.

Remember that when you partake in sufferings, He also partakes thereto. You are not alone, He is not afar from you, all He needs from you is a talk. Have a talk with the Lord the God of hosts. The peace of God the Lord of hosts will abound in you.

If Hannah had not prayed, faith and had peace she could have destroyed her life, maybe that of the rival, may be the rival's children in order to be even, and may be walked away from her marriage. I must tell you now that there is prayer and faith that can turn any situation around.

Please don't kill anyone, you are a child of God and he told you not to be a killer. In the book of Exodus 20 13 *'you shall not kill'* it is important to note that the word used is shall and not may, it is peremptory. We are not given a choice, it must not be done. You are not even supposed to think about it, let alone suppress it. Once you do so you are late, you have murdered a person. These thoughts emanate from failure to use the correct approach; pray to God, have faith in Him and he shall fill your heart with His peace.

I say wipe away your tears now, don't wait to see with your eyes. Things have changed and you better change with them too, otherwise you will not please God. We owe it to ourselves to please God.

I wish to quote chapter 1 verse 18 *'And she said, 'Let your maidservant find favour in your sight. 'So the woman went her way and ate, and her face was no longer sad.'*

Need I say that Hannah was happy for the birth of a male child before she could even sleep with her husband?

Need I say that Hannah was free and happy, started eating like a pregnant women before she could even become pregnant?

The word of God reveals Hannah as a woman walking tall, homing before birth and after prayer. Hannah went her way. She ate. Her face was no longer sad for it was very sad prior prayer. She prayed, put on the attitude of faith and she was no longer a sad women.

Hannah did not wait for pregnancy to eat. She did not wait for any sign to stop being sad. Her conduct saddened her rival of course, I believe her husband did not understand her too, maybe led to believe that it was the power of his advice and plea, his love towards her. The attitude confused the whole family.

The attitude you employ matters. Your attitude is so much in line with your action, for faith without works is dead. See the word of God in the book of James 2 verse14. James 2 verse 20 and James 2 verse 26. It is in this book where the issue of faith without works is over-emphasized. One is regarded as a foolish man if one has faith without works.

If you are a job applicant send as many applications as you possibly can for the job you need. Otherwise your faith will not serve you.

Let's consider Hannah and her rival again, this time taking a different approach. How often do we talk about the Devil, in our daily talks, prayers and prayer meetings. The Devil receives too much audience in our lives, more by Christians than non-Christians. Hannah did not make mention of her rival in her prayer. She did not entertain her rival. The Devil wants attention and if we give it to him he will put us under arrest. We will fear him than God. We will feel him and think that he has too much power over us. The Devil is such as Mr Nobody to us. Discard him from your mind. His loss is not fresh but old, our victory is not fresh too, and we earned it long time ago. It was won by Jesus Christ.

We are to talk about Jesus Christ of Nazareth, the son of the living God, the Lord of hosts. Preach Jesus and not the rival. Is it not amazing how Hannah dealt with her rival? She made time with God, in her petition there was no mention of her rival. The rival reaped no fame from the situation, the rival reaped no time from her situation, and the rival reaped neither audience nor name from it. Remember with the rival there is no such a thing called bad publicity. Publicity is publicity.

THE OUTCOMES OF HANNAH'S ATTITUDE

Hannah, the barren women became the mother of the prophet, a prophet of God the Lord of hosts, she received a son from the Lord of hosts and named him Samuel. Samuel means God has heard. What a name, God heard the day she prayed and not the day she fell pregnant or gave birth, no!

Samuel replaced Eli. Samuel served in the house of the Lord of hosts from childhood to death. Customarily Levites served from the age of 25 to 50. *See Numbers 4:3;* and *8:24-26.* God is not limited and cannot be limited by anything. The power of God erodes protocols. Faith knows no limitations. Faith is like a river in summer days. It flows with power and whatever stands on its way is taken out and away. Faith is powerful.

Hannah, who was barren, became a mother of six children. I Samuel 2 verse 21, says that *'And the Lord visited Hannah, so that she conceived and bore three sons and two daughters. Meanwhile the child Samuel grew before the Lord'.*

Hannah, who was mocked for her barrenness became joyful, prayed again but this time with joy and pride in the Lord of hosts, sung confidently and this time it was loud, she prayed with a smile, she despised pride. *See chapter 2 verse 1 to 11.*

Hannah, a women of wisdom, she did not go after her rival and sang a song to her but God. She had no time for her rival, she would rather spend time with God for a solution, once received, spend another time singing praises to God. Unlike some Christians, they even sing about the Devil, what a waste of time. They compose songs about the Devil; sing new songs about the Devil. He enjoys them despite the words. It is enough for him to receive audience, time and a song. That is too good for him. We must desist from doing so. It is bad. Hannah sung a new song to the Lord of hosts. Needles to say that she retained her peace and received more from God. Remember she worked for all of these through prayer, faith and the type of attitude she put on. The attitude of faith.

Hannah enjoyed the fulfillment of the prophesy by the prophet of the Lord of hosts Isaiah, it is recorded in the book of *Isaiah 54 that a barren should sing instead for her descendants will inherit the nations, and make desolate cities inhabited.*

Coming to think of it, don't you think Hannah needed the challenge she went through? I think it was not oversize, look at how she handled it socially and by faith? This challenge did not eat her up and or destroyed the family her husband set up. Her rival was fighting with herself and not with Hannah. The mocking propelled and ferried Hannah to her heights, there she was with great joy. If the rival only knew, she would not have done what she did? Do you think the Devil would do all the troubles if he knew more? Would he have killed Jesus if he knew? Our rivals are very important, let them live and let them function, they are like bacteria. We need them, don't we? Look at the promotion she got as a result. The very same challenges that we so much want to wish away are the building blocks of our lives and hence faith. The word of God says that *'knowing that the testing of your faith produces patience,'* in the book of James 1 verse 3.

CONCLUSION

With God, you will receive more, whatever you receive is better and greater, even permanent. Seek from God, achieve it God's way for your peace of mind. It will be fun and nice if its existence is not connected to a human being but God. We all know what people are capable of, in fact they are mortal. They change with weather; they don't have mercy like our God. When you mistake her she takes it back or tells the group that if it was not for her you would not have been where you are.

In order to achieve it God's way ask from Him, believe that whatever you have asked for you have received, act such as a person in possession already, then you will see with your naked eyes. Don't forget to praise

Him for that, sing for Him, to Him and about Him. Sing Him a new song; did you know that our God asked for a new song? Sing Him a new song. The attitude of faith.

I say please attitudinize!!!

www.ingramcontent.com/pod-product-compliance
Ingram Content Group UK Ltd.
Pitfield, Milton Keynes, MK11 3LW, UK
UKHW040020200726
13854UKWH00001B/282

9 781504 935722